HOW TO WORK WITH YOUR
CHAKRAS

A dynamic investigation that integrates scientific
findings on the aura with the esoteric teachings of the
mystery schools of the Great White Brotherhood.

What the great adepts have done,
you too can do—by learning to control your aura
through the science of the spoken Word.

T0021273

HOW TO WORK WITH YOUR
CHAKRAS

The Missing Dimension in Well-Being

ELIZABETH CLARE PROPHET

SUMMIT UNIVERSITY PRESS®

Gardiner, Montana

The Summit Lighthouse
63 Summit Way, Gardiner, MT 59030
Tel: 406-848-9500
www.SummitLighthouse.org
www.ElizabethClareProphet.com

Library of Congres Control Number: 2021932750
ISBN: 978-1-60988-360-7
ISBN: 978-1-60988-361-4 (eBook)

SUMMIT UNIVERSITY 🌱 PRESS®

Disclaimer and Notes: (1) The violet flame and the information in this book are not intended to replace qualified advice of professionals licensed in the fields of physical and mental health, finance or law. No guarantee is made by Summit University Press that the practices or meditations described in this book will necessarily yield successful results. The practice and proof of the science of being rests with the individual. (2) We consider God to be both masculine and feminine and therefore refer to the Father-Mother God. However, we have sometimes referred to God as he or him for readability and simplicity in the text.

24 23 22 21   1 2 3 4

CONTENTS

INTRODUCTION

Prana. Liquor Vitae. L-fields. Glowing auras. Kirlian photographs.

Centuries of research and speculation have finally documented the existence of the aura—a forcefield long acknowledged and used by adepts in the esoteric traditions. In this book, we consider how we can control the vibrating energy of our aura through the science of the spoken Word.

When we can see the background of scientific proof that the aura exists and that there are fundamental principles or laws governing the interaction of this energy, we can understand how the science of the spoken Word can affect the aura. We can then take that science and use it in a creative way for healing, blessing, and fulfilling the needs of life upon earth.

Our first step in this understanding is to expand our awareness of what we are—to see ourselves as identities suspended in time and space. Identities consisting of many interpenetrating forcefields—all vibrating at different frequencies. These frequencies are infinite, extending across the whole spectrum of consciousness.

THE AURA THROUGH THE AGES

The concept of a universal energy field interpenetrating our bodies is foundational to the teachings of the East. In the Hindu tradition, the word *prana* means "life-energy," coming from the root *pra*, "forth," and *an,* "to breathe." Prana is universal energy pulsating in and out of our bodies through the breathing process.

Yogic philosophy maintains that currents of prana radiate out of us as an aura around our physical bodies indicating our state of health, emotion, mind, and spirit. According to Eastern tradition, the aura can be used as a magnet to attract desired vibrations or to project currents of healing energy outward to any distance.

Ancient cultures in Egypt, Peru, the Yucatan, Israel, and throughout the world have spoken about a universal life energy analogous to prana. In China for thousands of years they have had the concept of *ch'i,* which persists to this day. It is said in Chinese medical philosophy "that ch'i is in the flow of blood and lymph and nervous impulses which follows well-defined pathways called meridians. According to the Chinese explanation, whenever the flow of this energy along the meridians is either obstructed or weakened, the likelihood for sickness is increased. It is proposed that we all exist suspended in a sea of energy which permeates between and through our body cells."[1]

In the fourth century B.C., Hippocrates made reference to the *enomron,* invisible emanations. He "wondered if a part of the natural healing force is a healing energy found in all organisms and in the air they breathe."[2]

Paracelsus, considered to be the father of anesthesia and modern chemistry, and the discoverer of the sympathetic nervous system, believed that the stars and planets influenced not only magnets but also the sympathetic nervous system. He claimed that this astrological influence was carried out through a subtle emanation or fluid that pervaded all of space. His practice of medicine included the concept of the *archaeus,* or universal essence, which composed the invisible body of all beings. The invisible body—subtle, ethereal, all-pervading—was seen as the blueprint and counterpart of the physical body.

If we glance to the yogic teachings of the East, we see how Paracelsus reached the same idea about the etheric or subtle body described in these ancient texts. Paracelsus described the visible world as the microcosm that was the reflection of the macrocosm. The essence of the microcosm was contained in the *Liquor Vitae,* the vital "fluid which contained the nature, quality, character, and essence of all beings."[3]

From this concept we can begin to see that by the control and use of this emanating energy field, we can affect the world around us because of the identical character of our life essence and the microcosm.

In the century that followed, a Flemish physician, Jon Baptista van Helmont, envisioned a "universal fluid" that pervaded all of nature, interpenetrating man's body and able to act on the mass of the universe.

Van Helmont, an alchemist with ties to the mystery school of his era, is regarded today as the father of biochemistry and the founder of the modern principles of disease and their cure. He was intrigued by the forces of magnetism and described them as "occult influences which bodies often exert toward each other at a distance whether by attraction or impulse."[4]

Practicing medicine in Vienna in the eighteenth century, Dr. Franz Anton Mesmer was to have a profound effect on the fields of science and medicine of his day and to the present. He taught that man was affected by the planets and stars through the medium of an energy field that acted as a fluid because it flowed in, around, and through all of Matter. He said that "everything in the universe is contiguous by means of a universal fluid in which all bodies are immersed."

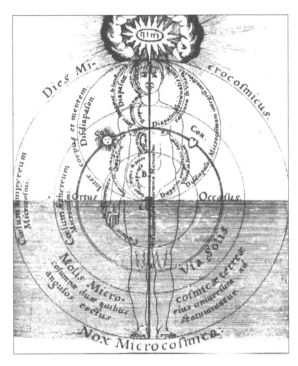

Seventeenth-century hermetic sketch shows the interrelationship of man the microcosm with God the Macrocosm. The heart corresponds to the Central Sun of man's being. The Tetragrammaton shown above man's head is signified by the Hebrew letters *YOD, HE, VAU, HE,* the mystical and "unpronounceable" Hebrew name of God.

Mesmer discovered that "all things in nature possess a particular power, which manifests itself by special actions on other bodies."[5] He found that he could control and direct emanations of energy to his patients, either nearby or at a great distance, and that this action would result in miraculous cures of the diseased. He experimented with the use of this healing energy resident within us and found that the power of sound could act to increase the strength of the healing currents.

The healing power of the purified aura was clearly demonstrated by Jesus Christ who often cured by the raising of his hand and the speaking of the fiat "Be thou made whole." But the power of his aura alone was enough to heal those who had pushed through the crowds to touch his garment or to get closer to his forcefield.

Mary Magdalene kneels before the master Jesus, aglow with a radiant light of the resurrection. His aura was so intense that many people were cured by merely touching the hem of his garment. Mary had experienced the power of Jesus' aura first-hand when he cast out of her seven possessing demons.

THE AURA UNVEILED

Eventually, in an attempt to understand its nature, scientists began to devise methods of observing this dynamic forcefield surrounding each of us. In the late 1800s, a medical electrician and member of London's Royal College of Surgeons, Walter J. Kilner, published a book based on four years of hospital experiments—*The Human Aura*. In this book he speculated that the magnetic radiations described by Mesmer might be perceptible only to sensitive people because the radiation might belong to a frequency outside the octave of normal sight.

Designing a process to make the aura visible, Kilner constructed screens of black glass for his subjects to look at for periods of time. His theory was that looking at the black screen for long periods increased the sensitivity of the night-seeing "rods" of the retina, enabling the person to see shorter wavelengths than normal. As a result of this training of the eyes, many people were able to see an auric field. The aura they described contained three definite zones superimposed upon each other and extending outward several feet from the body.

The size and the coloration of the aura seemed to vary according to the sex, age, mental ability, and the specific health of the subject. Kilner discovered that the aura appeared faint and obscure during illness. He formulated an elaborate system of medical diagnosis based upon the coloration and characteristics of the patient's aura. Modern research is supplying corroborating evidence for Kilner's findings on the aura.[6]

At Yale University, Dr. Harold Saxon Burr, professor of anatomy and biology, spent thirty years studying the energy emanations of man and plants. He was assisted by Dr. L. J. Ravitz, a psychiatrist. Together they found that all organisms are electrodynamic systems with a unique electromagnetic blueprint, or signature. They call this voltage pattern the "L-field," or "field of life," and correlated it with differences in human emotion, health, disease, and aging. They used closely monitored scientific methods and established that disorders in health definitely corresponded to shrinkages in the extension of the L-field. They also found that man not only exhibited specific energy field characteristics of his own, but that his forcefield interacted with the prevailing electromagnetic state of the environment.

In 1939 Semyon Kirlian and his wife Valentina, two amateur Russian photographers, discovered a photographic process whereby dynamic, colorful rays and emanations could be seen coming from the edges of plants as well as from the human body. Russian scientists later declared that the "bioluminescence" in the pictures was caused by a "biological plasma body," which they took to be analogous to the etheric body described by the ancients.

THE INFINITE SPECTRUM

Nikola Tesla, one of the greatest scientific geniuses of all time, invented the first alternating-current motor in existence, and he designed sources of unlimited energy that if put to use would have totally solved the energy problem long ago.

According to one of his biographers: "On that fateful afternoon in Budapest in 1882, when he was given the vision of the rotating magnetic field, there had come with it an illumination that revealed to him the whole cosmos, in its infinite variations as a symphony of alternating current. For him, the harmonies were played on a scale of electrical vibrations of a vast range in octaves. In one of the lower octaves was a single note, the 60-cycle-per-second alternating current, and on one of the highest octaves was visible light with its frequency of billions of cycles per second."[7]

Tesla's vision of continuous spectrums of currents in vibration expands our vision of the infinite variety of material form. Vibrations can range from billionths of a cycle per second to one cycle in a billion years. Infinity extends endlessly in both directions of the spectrum. We might say that our experience in this octave is the catching of a drop of this spectrum of the infinity of our own being infinite in all directions.

Man, the great reflection of God—made in his image and after his likeness—contains a certain potential of the Godhead in the blueprint of his being. The infinite spectrum of God's consciousness is accessible to those who choose to purify their vessels —that is, to make the vessels of consciousness consonant with the frequencies, the pure frequencies that are on this spectrum of infinity.

One of the many spiritual healers who had access to these vibrations was Henry Olcott, the founder and president of the Theosophical Society. For a period of several years, Olcott was the vehicle for miraculous cures of thousands of people—blind, paralyzed, deaf, and dumb. He explains in his writings that spiritual masters would often superimpose their auras over his own to effect the healing process in the patients. Many patients would describe how they saw the image and forcefield of the masters as the action took place. We can learn from this that as we become attuned to the auras of the masters, we can be increasingly powerful vehicles for doing their works upon earth.

2

BROTHERS OF LIGHT

We know that there are cosmic beings, light emanations of the Godhead, who concentrate the frequencies of God's energy, distributing this energy through their own auric forcefields. These illumined, enlightened beings—archangels, Elohim, ascended masters—have chosen by free will to allow their auras to be distributing centers of light throughout cosmos.

These are the beings of light we refer to when we speak of the Great White Brotherhood—those who make their auras available universally to every part of life as instruments of spiritual energies. For these energies can be lowered into the Matter universe only by the conscious decision of an individual to embody the Word—the tone or vibration of God's energy.

By association with their auric emanations, people have become familiar with the qualities embodied by the various archangels. When we contact the aura of Archangel Michael, we feel his tremendous power, his love of God's will, his faithfulness in service, his protection, his great God-determination to seal the planet Earth in its blueprint, in its divine plan, and to defend all life striving to become one with that divine plan. When we decide that we would like to be an extension of his God-free being, we meditate upon his sacred name. And then we give a mantra that transfers to us all of his momentum of thousands of years of devotion. (Mantra to Archangel Michael in chapter 3.)

As we begin to intone his Word through his mantra, the forcefield of his aura and our aura can become congruent. We can fuse our soul with the master, and master and disciple can become one whirling forcefield of energy.

So if it is Archangel Michael whose love we desire to manifest, we then become a part of the chain of hierarchy, the order of gurus and chelas that begins in the heart of God and descends to Archangel

Michael and all of the angels who serve in his bands. While we are meditating upon his flame and his mantra, we have a connection to an intricate hierarchy of light that spans the Spirit and the Matter cosmos. We have become a part of an infinite filigree of light emanations ensouled by beings who have chosen to be that Word; hence, they are the embodiment of the Word, or the Word incarnate— not necessarily meaning incarnate as flesh and blood, but embodying a facet of the Word at their level of consciousness.

When you think of this electric-blue pattern of lace spanning a cosmos on this one frequency, and then you think of an infinity of other frequencies of other levels of consciousness, you can suddenly see that the entire cosmos is a vibrating, quivering forcefield of interpenetrating auras.

We are all a part of this vast symphony of life, and by changing the dial of consciousness we can become suddenly aware of the Buddhas and bodhisattvas who embody and ensoul the essence of the crown chakra of God. Thus the recitation of their mantra gives to us attunement with their particular frequency.

3

THE CONTROL OF THE AURA
THROUGH THE
SCIENCE OF THE SPOKEN WORD

With the science of the spoken Word, this union with the masters' auras is precisely what occurs. As we give incisive invocations in the form of decrees to the ascended masters for help in solving specific problems, these beings of light place their auras, or their electronic forcefield, not only over the decreer but also over the problem itself.

The Brotherhood then sets up a polarity between the decreer and the problem, and an oscillation of light occurs between the two. As the light goes back and forth, there is an interchange of energy. The master's blueprint superimposed over the decreer absorbs and transmutes the negative energy in the condition upon which the decreer is focusing.

In this way, all use of dynamic decrees is the scientific use of the light of the aura. The rhythm and vibrational patterns of mantras and decrees act upon our pranic currents by bringing this fluid, or life energy, into harmony with the pattern of the decree. As we begin to intone these decrees or mantras written by the masters, our auras then take on the inner blueprint of the Word of the master.

The Word of the master is his identity, and his identity is a unique blueprint. If we desire to absorb from him his virtues, his God consciousness, his light, we must allow our own inner blueprint to become superimposed by the inner blueprint of the master during our period of meditation.

This we do by free will, for this is the meaning of discipleship—to become the Incarnate Word of the master. And we become his Word by the recitation of his mantra. We as the cup, the receiver, absorb the maximum light we can contain of the master's consciousness—according to our meditation, our concentration, and our attunement with his inner blueprint.

HARMONY: THE STARTING POINT

The foundation of the entire exercise of the spoken Word and the influence or control of the aura is harmony—harmony within one's entire force-field. Harmony is never mechanical. It is not simply the proper arrangement of the dots of consciousness. Harmony is truly the manifestation of divine love. Where there is not love, there cannot be true harmony. This is why all the great avatars of the ages have taught us that the fundamental principle of all true religion is divine love.

From the foundation of love and the establishment of harmony, we begin the meditation upon the Godhead that harmonizes our own inner blueprint. With harmony in our own being, it becomes easier then to attune to the harmony of God-free beings, to establish their blueprint by a simple act of devotion before the God flame that they have magnified in their being. Then we can begin the intonation of the mantra that scientifically transfers their presence to our own.

Since the essence of prana does extend and permeate all of Matter, we can understand how by the spoken Word we can not only imprint energy with a healing pattern but we can also send it out into a world in need of healing. When you think that with the science of the spoken Word you can become such a sending station of light, you begin to realize that the circles of man's influence for good are truly infinite.

We influence every person and every blade of grass on the planet, every particle of the oceans and the skies to the very core of the earth, to the next galaxy... and beyond.

When you desire to contact the transcendent power, faith, and determination of Archangel Michael, close your eyes, center in your heart, and visualize a blazing white sphere of light over your physical heart. You are now ready to invoke the pure energy of God into your aura and world.

As God through you affirms the decree, "Blue Lightning Is Thy Love," Archangel Michael places his forcefield over you, drawing you into an infinite filigree of light spanning the Spirit/Matter cosmos —a filigree composed of all those beings of light who long ago determined to become the Word incarnate. With Jesus, theirs is the mantra, *I AM the light of the world.*

Blue Lightning Is Thy Love!

In the name of the beloved mighty victorious Presence of God, I AM in me, my very own beloved Holy Christ Self, Holy Christ Selves of all mankind, beloved Archangel Michael and his legions of blue-lightning angels, the entire Spirit of the Great White Brotherhood and the World Mother, I decree:

> 1. Blue lightning is thy love
>   Flood forth to free all!
>   Blue lightning is thy power
>   In God I see all!
>   Blue lightning is thy mind
>   In pure truth I find!

Light will overcome
Light will make us one
Light from blue-fire sun
Command us now all free!

2. Blue lightning is thy law
Blaze forth as holy awe!
Blue lightning is thy name
Our heart's altar do enflame!
Blue lightning maketh free
In God I'll ever be!

Light will overcome
Light will make us one
Light from blue-fire sun
Command us now all free!

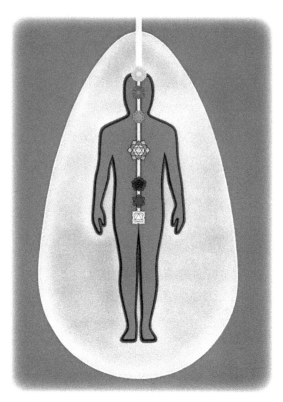

Fig. 1.   Through the science of the spoken Word you can infuse your auric egg with the light of the cosmos and become a powerful sending station for God's healing energy to your family and community.

4

YOUR AURIC EGG

In order to take part in this magnificent symphony of life benefiting life, you must understand the basic forcefield with which you work when you use the science of the spoken Word—your auric egg (Fig. 1). This is a simplified drawing of your auric egg intact, unviolated, in its purest manifestation, showing the etheric body with the chakras aligned. This shows that there are seven major centers of light, and from these centers there come forth the light emanations that compose the layers upon layers of the fabric of the aura.

The seven centers mark seven planes of vibration. Within each of those planes there is an infinite succession of frequencies that make up a single color band. Even in the narrow spectrum of our own eyesight, we realize that within the range of blue or green or pink there are many vibrations.

And so, what seems to be a simple concept of seven rays actually spans infinity.

According to our attunement with the Godhead and with the light, we can experience with increasing sensitivity these planes of being. As we experience them and meditate upon them, they flow through us, and the aura reflects the rainbow rays of that meditation and oneness. So you might say that these seven centers represent the opportunity for us to lower into manifestation that certain portion of the infinity of the Godhead that is assigned to man as the boundaries of his habitation in time and space.

From the envelope of light within your auric egg —which becomes a very concentrated white-fire cloud of energy—you begin to expand the aura.

The idea of meditation is to contact a high forcefield of God's energy, to draw it around one's self, and to make it the very platform for the use of the dynamic decree. When the Word is spoken without the resonating board, so to speak, of this auric egg, it has far less influence to penetrate the Matter spheres. But if by love and harmony and meditation upon God you establish this forcefield of intense white light, then you have the ability of the instrument of the aura to project God's healing love outward from where you are.

The most effective use of the science of the spoken Word occurs when the person who uses it recognizes that he is only the instrument of the Higher Mind of God, or of those who have become one with God—the ascended masters. When the individual considers himself to be the source of the mantra or somehow the one who controls the mantra, then he actually limits his ability for the Source of the mantra to flow through him—the great manus of the races, the avatars, the Buddhas, and the Cosmic Christs. So the use of the science of the Word without the Great Cause—God himself behind the effect—is self-limiting by its very nature.

YOUR AURA AND YOUR REAL SELF

This Chart of Your Divine Self (Fig. 2) shows the Great God Self individualized as the cause behind the effect of all life. The concentric rings are a pattern of what the human aura is intended to be like. Your auric forcefield can be a sphere of light as large as you will it. And its light emanations from the center of the heart outward should follow this blueprint of the upper spheres, the seven color bands including the white light.

The goal of the path of initiation under the ascended masters is to establish that giant forcefield of God consciousness around the aura of the lower figure in the Chart, which is you in the state of evolution in this octave.

This is the light of God, the light of cosmos. And because its frequency is so intense, it cannot come upon the human without annihilating that human. And for this cause, God sent into the world his only begotten Son, the Christ, who has been embodied in avatars for hundreds of thousands of years.

You have a personal Christ who is mediator between you and this great dynamo of generating light and God consciousness. Through the heart of the Mediator, the central figure in the Chart, you receive just that portion of light that you are able to contain in the lower octaves because of your own level of vibration. Your vibration, your state of mind and feeling, determines how much of that light you can hold.

Fig. 2.   The Chart of Your Divine Self depicts your individualized God Self surrounded by seven spheres of light focusing seven planes of God consciousness. Standing between you here on earth and this magnificent God Self is your personal Christ—your Real Self. Our goal is to raise our consciousness to the level of this Real Self and become one with our I AM Presence.

This Christ Self is your Real Self. Until you can establish the awareness of who your Real Self is, you—as a soul moving toward the alchemical marriage with the Divine Whole—are the student under your own real Christ-identity.

And so you are aware of yourself as a separate person from that Christ Self and you are a separate person as long as you are vibrating at a level of human incompleteness or imperfection.

The more you become a student of your inner Guru, the more the mirror of your mind and aura will reflect that person. Therefore, meditation upon the personal Christ through the archetype of the Son of God manifest in Jesus Christ or Saint Germain or Lord Krishna or Elijah or Elisha translates to us the nature of our own Real Self. You may go for years or centuries or embodiments as the student of your Christ consciousness until you so reflect that consciousness that the middle figure in the Chart draws closer and closer and soon there is no longer a separation of two identities but there is only one.

Jesus was born with a full conscious awareness of his Christ-identity. And so he was called Jesus the Christ—Jesus, the Anointed One, the one anointed with his real person. When you then become the fullness of that person, you are called the Word incarnate.

Our goal is to discover the mystery of the Word incarnate—to understand that love, which is the key to that mystery, is a science. Love is not simply a feeling that we have for one another. Behind that feeling is the entire science of being. Through love we are fused once again to the inner reality; through love the soul can then become a permanent atom in the being of God.

Jesus walked the earth as that Christ Self and Mediator; therefore he stood as the Mediator for all people between their human consciousness and the great dazzling sun of Reality whom he addressed as the Father. During his mission as the Word incarnate, Jesus became a direct contact with that mighty I AM Presence for all living on earth. His body could contain an extraordinary portion of that light.

Many people have so much density that they cannot even contact their own Real Self or their own Mediator. Therefore they must go to someone who is the Word incarnate until they can reestablish through that Guru their tie to their own God Presence.

This is the first step on the path of initiation. People do not automatically have contact with their I AM Presence or their Christ Self. If they did, they would be leading entirely different lives than they do today. What spans the gap between their density and their Christ Self is the mantra. The moment that you begin to recite a mantra you are in contact with one who has become the Word incarnate. Instantaneously, you receive a transfer of light.

5

THE POWER OF LIGHT

The very fact that there is the manipulation of Matter by witchcraft or black magic or satanic rite, which is a complete perversion of the science of the spoken Word and yet seems to be powerful, should show us how infinitely more powerful is the creative Word when it is emitted in love and according to the real laws of the universe. This, then, is precisely what the teachings of the ascended masters are all about.

The reason the ascended masters have been knocking at our door for a century is to get through to us that we do not have to sit and be covered over by the auric emanations that surround the planet—that we do not have to be the victims of the auric emanations we have created in past ages and thereby continue on a downward spiral. The masters are telling us that by the alchemy of the Word itself we can change our life. We can increase our responses to higher vibrations of light.

It's exciting to consider that this is a path of free will, that millions of beings who are advanced beyond us on this Path have chosen to tarry with earth and her evolutions to help us to accelerate our evolution. It's exciting to realize that every part of God in the universe has the opportunity to exercise the free will to become more of God.

Think of the many people upon this planet who do not know that simple truth and then you can understand why there is such great darkness, why there is war, unequal distribution of the abundant life, and all of the problems we face.

For good or for ill we can influence the cosmos. When we decree together, not only our individual aura but our whole planet can become charged with the light of the Brotherhood. We are vibrating with infinite light, and by our conscious contact with God and our exercise of free will, we can also do anything with this light. This is what the real awakening of this final portion of the twentieth century is all about.

It's exciting to live and to experiment in the laboratory of our own cosmic egg and to know that this laboratory expands and expands and expands. What can be done with Matter through the aura and the spoken Word lies before us as a vast discovery and an exploration.

6

KIRLIAN PHOTOGRAPHY

This unique photographic method captures one small band of the many levels of vibration composing the human aura.

Kirlian photograph of fingertips 1

The left photograph shows the fingertips of a couple extremely defensive toward one another. If you look closely, you can see an energy barrier between the two fingers. The photograph on the right shows the same couple thinking loving thoughts. Notice energy arcing between them.

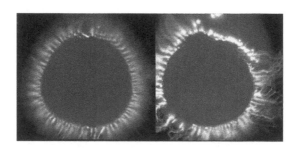

Kirlian photograph of fingertips 2

The above photographs show a non-smoker's fingertip (left) compared to that of a smoker (right).

Kirlian photograph of leaves

On the left four leaves placed in a symmetrical pattern reveal the auric emanation in the blueprint of the leaves.

The photograph on the right illustrates the famous phantom leaf effect. The energy pattern still exists after the physical tip of the leaf has been removed—giving documentary proof of a blueprint existing in a dimension beyond the physical. Kirlian photographs are from *Rainbows of Life* by Mikol Davis and Earle Lane, Harper Colophon Books.

7

AN EXERCISE IN
TONING THE CHAKRAS

"The Fitness Craze," "Body Beautiful," "America in Training." How many headlines have you read about the benefits of physical exercise?

The current trends would have you believe that almost any problem you can think of can be cured through some sort of workout program. Books, magazines, and television shows abound, touting everything from aerobics to racquetball as the ultimate remedy for a wide range of maladies from simple stress to heart disease.

Health, as we all know, is a product of proper diet, positive mental attitude, enough sleep, and physical exercise—right? Well, maybe. . . .

While such activities are definitely valid, there has been a consistent omission of a very important element. The missing dimension in physical fitness has nothing to do with what we normally think of as health-promoting factors.

What we are talking about are centers of energy flow within your body that you cannot see or touch but that are as important to isolate and condition as your triceps. These centers are called chakras—the Sanskrit word meaning "wheel" or "disc." There are seven major chakras within your body.

You're probably wondering how in the world something you can't even see, let alone exercise, can be so important to fitness! Well, you *can* exercise your chakras. And even if you can't see them, you can feel them. More on this later.

8

THE FOUR LOWER BODIES

To begin with, the physical body of an athlete is only one-quarter of the whole person. You have your mental body (your thoughts and cognitive mind), your emotional body (feelings and desires), and your etheric body (your memory, containing layers of the subconscious and the superconscious mind as well as the blueprint of life) to train for the optimum performance in any situation—be it track, court, or gridiron.

These three other "bodies" fulfill a very important role in any athletic training program. It is they that support the physical body and give it that extra determination to push through, to work those muscles, even when—and especially when—you feel that "burn" that lets you know you are making progress.

As anyone familiar with the world of physical fitness can testify, workouts are grueling and painful, and exact a heavy toll on the body. Except for a possible endorphin-induced high, there is little immediate physical gratification. (Endorphins are chemicals produced by the body during periods of intense exertion that mimic the effects of opium on the brain. They contribute largely, along with pain-blocking enkephalins, to the phenomenon known as "runner's high.")

Another phenomenon known to many runners is the "wall." This is the point at which the body has used up all of its available glycogen and has no more energy to give to the muscles. Usually this is after twenty miles or so, when the body is physically exhausted.

Sometimes drinking sugar water during the run will combat this problem. Most people, however, will get "exhausted" long before the wall is reached. For those who do not run regularly, to actually go twenty miles would be impossible without risking serious injury.

The point I am making here is that there are many who *could* run the twenty miles but stop at six or ten because they think or feel that they can't do it. If those people would get their mental and emotional bodies working with their physical, they would excel. This is only common sense.

Any gratification achieved through a fitness program is delayed. Be it drinking a glass of apple juice and taking a cool shower after the evening's program or long-term muscular gain, the joy of a workout is not the workout itself.

Consequently, unless you are one who enjoys pain, there must be other factors driving you to put your body through its paces. These could be your *memories* of how good you felt last time you "pumped iron," your *mental* determination to excel, or the desire to attain the *emotional* control that comes with the true mastery of any sport or martial art.

Take, for example, the case of John McEnroe, the tennis pro who plays a very good game but has been known to throw his racquet and berate the judges. His actions reveal a temporary absence of emotional control for which he receives no small amount of bad publicity.

In the 1980 Davis Cup tournament in Buenos Aires, McEnroe was badly beaten. This was due in large part to the clay courts on which the games were played. Sullen and dejected, McEnroe broke his routine by remaining unusually quiet for the duration of the competition.

But even this despondency is a lack of emotional control. If McEnroe had really wanted to win that tournament, he would have had to maintain a positive attitude while at the same time keeping his lid on. This is the middle path of the Buddha—just enough of the right qualities at the right time, without ever losing control.

In any event, anyone will probably play a much better game, as well as increase their popularity immensely, if they would integrate their "emotional body" with their physical.

Tennis, or even racquetball, requires a great deal of memory in addition to emotional control. Just think of the countless hours of practice McEnroe has spent. Not only must he have developed his forearm and trained his eye, but also he must re-member with intimate detail which type of shot to use on what occasion and the exact angle of inci-dence and reflection of every ball that screams over the net and into his court.

Once memorized in every cell, these responses must then become automated—like a bio-electric formula invoked and executed faster than the "mind" can think.

As far as mental attitude is concerned, this is mainly being "psyched up" for the game. No mat-ter how skilled your opponent, or what the playing surface is composed of, you must know you have the ability and determination to win.

All right, you say, what does all of this have to do with your chakras? Thought you'd never ask!

Each body is separate and distinct—sharing, or intersecting through, the common coordinates of the seven chakras. In the physical, they are specifi-cally attached through the central nervous and endocrine systems. The chakras are the central vehicles for the flow of light from your soul to your four bodies.

In order to maximize your potential, you must have a clear passage for the light and energy you receive from the Life Source each day to move freely through all of your bodies. If any chakra is clogged, it can throw one or more of your four bodies out of alignment. If one of the four lower bodies is out of alignment, you can't make the most of any of them.

All the push-ups in the world won't mean a thing if you are still fighting your own sense of limitation. Therefore, it behooves anyone who is really serious about fitness and well-being to study and know the chakras and their effects on training as well as all aspects of everyday life.

9

THE "SPINNING WHEELS" OF THE YOGI

In Indian yogic tradition, the seven centers of spiritual energy—*chakras* ("wheels") or *padmas* ("lotuses")—act as the organs of the subtle body of man. Situated along the spinal column and invisible to the physical eye, the chakras store, transform, and distribute the vital force that flows through them to every part of the body.

This vital force (prana) is carried through the body by a network of threadlike, luminous vessels *(nadis)* that number in the thousands. Prana, in the strictest sense of the word, is equated with the qualities of breath, but in Indian philosophy it is considered to be the universal force or primal energy that sustains all physical and spiritual processes. Carl Jung has described it as "both the breath and the universal dynamics of the cosmos."

Of the fourteen principal energy channels, the three most prominent nadis are those around the spine. The left channel, *Ida* (the pale, lunar nadi), and the right channel, *Pingala* (the red, solar nadi), spiral in opposite directions around the central energy channel, *Sushumna,* that runs through the spinal column from the base of the spine to the brain. These three meet and then separate again between the eyebrows at the *Ajna* chakra, often portrayed as the "third eye" on images of the Hindu deities and the Buddha.

The goal of the yogi is to open the Sushumna, whose entrance at the lower end is blocked by what the *Tantras* call the Serpent Power (personified as the sleeping Goddess Kundalini, literally "coiled-up serpent") in the *Muladhara* chakra at the base of the spine.

The Kundalini (symbol of the dormant, innate powers of divinity) can be awakened in a number of ways—specific yogic techniques, spiritual disciplines, an intense love for God. When done with mastery and control by the yogi, it is a liberating force leading to heightened spiritual powers *(siddhis);*

when ignorantly or prematurely released, it is said to be dangerously destructive.

As the Kundalini ascends the Sushumna and penetrates one by one the chakras in the subtle body, the energies of each chakra are activated and assimilated by the Kundalini. The chakra begins to spin like a wheel and the lotus opens and raises her petals—signifying the unfoldment of latent powers. When the Kundalini reaches the seventh center, *Sahasrara*, the thousand-petaled lotus at the top of the head, the yogi experiences Illumination and *samadhi* (ecstasy, perfect union and identification with God).

There is an intricate symbology associated with each of the chakras. Early Indian scroll paintings often depict these centers as abstract energy vortices, but they are usually represented as lotus blossoms. The number and position of the nadis that emanate from each chakra give the appearance of a specific number of lotus petals.

Each petal is inscribed with a Sanskrit letter that "condenses" one or more mystic sounds *(mantras)* whose vibration corresponds to the subtle sounds made by the forces working in the chakra. The essential activity of the *tattva,* or element (earth, water, fire, air or ether), related to the chakra is denoted by the Sanskrit *bija* (seed syllable) at the center of the lotus.

In addition, each chakra governs a specific function of the body and has its own color, geometric form, animal representation, and presiding god and goddess (male and female polarity) that express the qualities of the element and principles associated with it.

10

THE HEART CHAKRA

The Threefold Flame of the Heart

The central and most important organ of your body is your heart. Likewise, the central and most important chakra is the heart chakra. It also contains the threefold flame.

The threefold flame is the blossoming of light within your heart, anchored there through the descent of the crystal cord. It is not really a flame like a candle, but we can think of it more in terms of the flame that "burned the bush and consumed it not." (Exod. 3:2) (See Chart of Your Divine Self, chapter 4, Fig. 2, p. 29.) The crystal cord is the thread of light that descends from your "I AM Presence," another name for your God Self.

Why is the flame in your heart called "three-fold"? Because it embodies the three God-qualities of power, wisdom, and love, also personified in the Trinity.

Ideally, these are kept in balance. But few have the mastery to do this. Instead, people fill their hearts with hatred, fear, and malice, which on the spiritual level resemble lead or asphalt. (Heart disease, though on the decline, remains the biggest killer in the country. Small wonder.)

One of the most important parts of keeping fit is cleaning up and balancing the heart chakra. Just as the brain and organs depend on blood flow, so all other chakras depend on energy flow from the heart. Thus, when the heart is clogged through selfishness and possessiveness, which blocks this flow, all of the chakras suffer.

Secondly, after the threefold flame is balanced, it must then be expanded. Before the proverbial Fall of man, the threefold flame surrounded the body completely and reached an approximate height of five to seven feet.

At that time, the crystal cord was over nine feet in diameter, channeling tremendous amounts of divine energy into the heart chakra of man. This increased his longevity—hence the extraordinarily long lifespans of such antediluvian figures as Methuselah and Noah—and enabled him to perform what would now be considered as superhuman feats.

Finally, the heart chakra must be protected. It is extremely sensitive to all types of vibrations, both good and bad. This sensitivity must be guarded.

Negative frequencies impinging upon the heart can cause heart attacks. Most dangerous are hatred, mental criticism, hardness of heart, envy, and even the death wish, which amounts to witchcraft. By failing to groom their thoughts and feelings with love, people actually engage in a mental and emotional malpractice against one another on a day-to-day basis.

LIGHT MANTRAS FOR THE HEART

Saint Germain, the master who is the keystone of the arch of the Aquarian age, has given us a mantra for the cleansing of our chakras. This mantra can be used in conjunction with all of the other mantras contained in this book. It is very simple and easy to remember and can be given out loud or "under your breath" at any time when things aren't going well or you feel a heaviness in your body or a burden on your heart.

I AM a being of violet fire,
I AM the purity God desires!

Similar in quality to the threefold flame in the heart, the violet fire, or violet flame, is specifically for the transmutation of negative karma, records of nonfulfillment in this or past lives, or negativity in any form.

It is the flame of freedom and of the Holy Spirit that forgives sin by dissolving its cause, effect, record, and memory. It is the God-energy that frees the atoms, cells, and electrons in your four lower bodies to sing the song of their fiery destiny. And it will liberate all who use it—mentally, psychologically, and spiritually.

Saint Germain's mantra for the Aquarian age can be adapted for use with all chakras as follows:

My heart is a chakra of violet fire,
My heart is the purity God desires!

My throat chakra is a wheel of violet fire,
My throat chakra is the purity God desires!

My solar plexus is a sun of violet fire,
My solar plexus is the purity God desires!

My third eye is a center of violet fire,
My third eye is the purity God desires!

My soul chakra is a sphere of violet fire,
My soul is the purity God desires!

My crown chakra is a lotus of violet fire,
My crown chakra is the purity God desires!

My base chakra is a fount of violet fire,
My base chakra is the purity God desires!

Simply give the mantra corresponding to the specific chakra you feel needs cleansing, and give it until you feel a release from your tension, anxiety or whatever problem you may have. Try it! It works.

For the purposes of visualization, the heart chakra, when at its optimum, emits a white fire clothed with shades of pink, rose, and ruby—depending on the intensity and purity of the love expressed.

This rose of the heart has twelve petals. It is visualized over the place of the physical heart, although in the perfected state, it and its physical counterpart would be in the center of the torso.

See the threefold flame within it, with its three plumes of power, wisdom, and love as flames of blue, gold, and pink respectively. As an added protection against world weight, you can see in your mind's eye a spinning disc of white light in front of the heart. For a real clearing action, give the "I AM Light" mantra.

When you say the mantra (or any mantra) aloud, you are setting up a forcefield of light around your heart. This forcefield will keep away the "bad vibes" and other assorted negative energies that tend, at times, to make things go wrong.

This is one of many practical applications of the science of the spoken Word. Through the correct use of the throat chakra in decrees such as this one, we effectively become co-creators with our higher consciousness. As spoken of in the Book of Job, "The Almighty shall be thy defence.... Thou shalt make thy prayer unto him, and he shall hear thee.... Thou shalt also decree a thing, and it shall be established unto thee: and the light shall shine upon thy ways." (Job 22:25, 27, 28)

"I AM" is the name of God as spoken to Moses: "Tell them, 'I AM' hath sent me unto you. This is my name for ever." (Exod. 3:14, 15) Therefore, when we affirm "I AM," we are affirming *"God in me is"* or *"God in me is the action of...."* Whatever follows—whether it be speech, prayer, mantra, or decree—it is self-realized because it is the power of God's name and his Be-ness that works creative change in our lives.

I AM Light

I AM light, glowing light,
Radiating light, intensified light.
God consumes my darkness,
Transmuting it into light.

This day I AM a focus of the Central Sun.
Flowing through me is a crystal river,
A living fountain of light
That can never be qualified
By human thought and feeling.
I AM an outpost of the Divine.
Such darkness as has used me is swallowed up
By the mighty river of light which I AM.

I AM, I AM, I AM light;
I live, I live, I live in light.
I AM light's fullest dimension;
I AM light's purest intention.
I AM light, light, light
Flooding the world everywhere I move,
Blessing, strengthening, and conveying
The purpose of the kingdom of heaven.

By meditating on the white fire surrounding the threefold flame in the secret chamber of your heart and giving the "I AM Light" mantra for the protection of the heart chakra, you are really benefiting all of your chakras.

As you know, oxygenated blood from the lungs must first pass through the heart before it can nourish the rest of the body. Similarly, the light from your I AM Presence must also pass through the heart. Whatever the heart contains is then carried to all the other chakras.

Saint Germain has also given us the following "Light of the Heart" mantra to carry the light of the heart to all of the chakras. Give it with joy, love, and immense gratitude for the gift of life.

> I AM the light of the heart
> Shining in the darkness of being
> And changing all into the golden treasury
> Of the mind of Christ.
>
> I AM projecting my love
> Out into the world
> To erase all errors
> And to break down all barriers.

I AM the power of Infinite Love,
Amplifying Itself
Until It is victorious,
World without end!

Indeed, the energy of the Life Source is the only real "fountain of youth" in existence. (Ironically, Ponce de Leon and countless others have spent a major portion of their lives chasing that flaming youth that was really in their heart.)

As a result of the misuse of this energy, the crystal cord is today a mere thread, and the threefold flame measures an average height of one-sixteenth of an inch. If we are ever to regain our former power and vitality, we must prove ourselves the master over what we now have.

VITALITY AND PRANA

As for vitality, it is the endless pursuit of this elusive quality that drives many fitness devotees to their efforts. The reason exercise is vitalizing in the first place is that it causes the increased intake of prana.

Prana is Sanskrit for "breath," but it is much more. Prana is life energy. It comes from God through many channels. The most reliable source of prana is clean air near moving water, charged with sunlight.

It can be postulated that the amount of prana in the air is a direct function of the concentration of negatively charged ions. (A negatively charged ion is an air molecule that is carrying an extra electron. Similarly, a positively charged ion has been stripped of an electron.)

I would not go so far as to say that prana *is* negatively charged ions, but let's just say that when the concentration of negative ions is naturally high, you can be reasonably sure there is some prana around.

Many studies have proven that the ion concentration in the air has a profound effect on the body. In working environments in the cities, positive ions that are detrimental to health are generated in quantity by central air-conditioning systems, pollution, and automobiles.

On the other hand, rain and lightning storms generate negative ions that benefit the body. The ocean, rivers, streams, and all types of vegetation also contribute to the negative ionization of the air.

When you run along the beach on a clear day, you are doing far more to revitalize your physical temple than if you were to jog for twice the time through the back streets of L.A. Once you take into consideration environmental factors, the where and when becomes as important as the how and for how long.

Since most of us do live in the city, it's important to find the time to go elsewhere—into nature, to clear out our physical bodies of pollution and processed food, cleanse our chakras through fasting, meditation, and mantras, and bring the other three bodies into alignment.

The intake of prana is extremely beneficial, as its effect is not limited to the physical. It passes to the three other bodies through channels called nadis and vitalizes your entire being.

11

THE THROAT CHAKRA

The Powerful Throat Center

The next center we should be concerned with is the throat chakra. It is located over the physical throat, has sixteen petals, and is blue in color. It is the power chakra, and through the talent of speech unique to man, it can release large quantities of energy, both good and bad.

Through the disciplined use of the spoken Word, we can make great progress in toning all of our chakras. With misuse—such as cursing in the name of God or Jesus Christ, gossip, criticism, sarcasm, angry words, or "unseemly conversation" —we do ourselves great harm as well as increase the planetary level of human effluvia.

Even irritation toward others and the voicing of that irritation causes imbalance within all of the chakras, because the throat is the command center through which our creative forces flow to all life, establishing the tenor of our aura and our person.

This concept is not new. Jesus admonished us, "Let your communication be, Yea, yea; and Nay, nay: for whatsoever is more than these cometh of evil." (Matt. 5:37) This was not meant to exclude necessary communication between persons but was a reminder to us of the seriousness of the misuse of the word; and it also revealed his awareness of the power of the spoken Word to affirm Truth.

Through the affirmation of Truth ("Yea, yea"), we channel it in action in our lives, and denying error ("Nay, nay"), we cast it out.

He also stated that "every idle word that men shall speak, they shall give account thereof in the day of judgment. For by thy words thou shalt be justified, and by thy words thou shalt be condemned." (Matt. 12:36, 37)

This shows that Jesus believed words were as important as actions, and that both would be weighed in the soul's ultimate evaluation. It's also important to realize that idle chatter (like idle sex) drains you of the energy you need to focus for maximum performance. Too much talk and not enough action, like any other indulgence, squanders the life force and reveals an absence of control and personal integration.

Despite its enormous significance in human relations, our society has de-emphasized the word to such a degree that cynicism and incisiveness have become more important than true communication.

Music is the barometer of society, and as the Scottish patriot Andrew Fletcher of Saltoun so aptly commented, "If a man were permitted to make all the ballads, he need not care who should make the laws of a nation."

Just tune in your radio to any popular station. Tell me if you can find four songs in a row where some aspect of life isn't being degraded. Everything is made common. Every action has a hidden motive. People are painted as having no sincerity in word or in deed.

Even words themselves cease to have meaning in the minds of many. People can lie, curse, gossip, and it's all justified matter-of-factly with "It's just words." The sad part is that, to many, words have become empty—something to use to manipulate others or to express anger.

Much of social interaction today is governed by the "cocktail party" mentality of one-upmanship— along with the couching of every aggressive statement in terms of some sort of joke or good humor so as to be able to hurt another deeply without "ruffling anyone's feathers."

And heaven forbid that the poor guy should take anyone seriously, lest he be greeted with more hoots of laughter and shouts of "Paranoid?" and "Can't take a joke?"

Generally, the way this is dealt with is that these "sophisticates" develop a razor-sharp tongue, ready to counter each rapier thrust of caustic wit with an even more incisive jab. Then everyone laughs and supposedly none are the worse for the wear.

But are they? What about the deep-seated scars that this inflicts on the unsuspecting and sensitive individual? What about the sincere seeker whose nature will not allow him to participate in this type of game? Is he to be cast out of society, branded a simpleton?

Certainly all of this is not what the throat chakra is meant for. When an individual is accustomed to hearing mostly innuendo and sarcasm from everyone around him, who should be surprised that he "doesn't listen any more"?

In our society, more than anything else, we need to realize the importance of the word. In our time, when communication has become all but automated, and computers "talk" to each other faster and more accurately than people, we think of technology as the cure for all of our ills.

Just look at the word *technology*. It comes from the Greek *techne,* meaning "art" or "craft," and *logos,* meaning "word." So here we are, in the *age of the art of the word,* and communication between individuals is one of our biggest problems!

David's prayer ought to become our own: "Let the words of my mouth and the meditation of my heart be acceptable in thy sight, O Lord, my strength and my redeemer." (Ps. 19:14)

If we all thought about what we said each time we said it as if we were speaking to or in front of God, our conversations would be quite different. This, then, is the first step to the clearing of the throat chakra: to purify our speech.

The very strength of God's will we misuse in this center can become the power to engage the cosmic law in our life. Try this mantra of Christ's victory in you:

> Not my will,
> Not my will,
> Not my will,
> But Thine be done!

It can even be used to maintain the rhythm of your exercise, mentally or verbally affirmed. Visualize the blue flame of life's blueprint working through your throat chakra and spoken Word to charge your body with the integrating will of the universe.

12

THE SOLAR-PLEXUS CHAKRA

The Place of the Sun

Complementing the throat, below the heart, is the solar-plexus chakra. It is located at the navel and corresponds to the nerve center there. It has ten petals and its colors are a combination of rich purple and metallic gold. When you become agitated and feel that familiar discomfort "in the pit of your stomach," you know that it is your solar plexus that has been affected.

This energy is usually released through the throat in the form of disruptive verbiage. The solar plexus and the throat are corresponding chakras, and when in harmony, the energies of both converge in the heart for peaceful and loving communication. When one or the other is in disharmony, both chakras are involved.

Many of our emotions are expressed through these two chakras. You will notice that under normal circumstances, when people are expressing feelings of love, kindness, or any other positive emotion, they usually speak in a quiet and resonant tone of voice. As soon as the solar plexus is agitated, however, the pitch and the volume go up. This is most noticeable when the person is in a state of anger or anxiety.

Mastering the solar plexus requires the mastery of our emotions by harnessing ourselves to the divine will—by the sacred fire of the heart. When they are controlled, we can begin the purification of this chakra through meditation and dynamic decrees.

While visualizing the chakra as shown, give "The Balm of Gilead." This prayer will help calm your emotions (your *energies in motion*) whenever you feel agitated or ill at ease.

> O love of God, immortal love,
> Enfold all in thy ray:
> Send compassion from above
> To raise them all today!
> In the fullness of thy power,
> Shed thy glorious beams
> Upon the earth and all thereon
> Where life in shadow seems!
> Let the light of God blaze forth
> To cut men free from pain:
> Raise them up and clothe them, God,
> With thy mighty I AM name!

The solar plexus is very much linked to the soul. Therefore, if this chakra is kept pure, you will be more in touch with your true feelings and self. Our emotions, magnifying the pure desire of the Higher Self, are intended to amplify the soul and the potential of the soul.

- 13 -

THE THIRD-EYE CHAKRA

The Inner Eye

Ascending once again above the heart, we find the third-eye chakra. This center is just as important to keep free of human debris as any of the other six—even more so, because it is the orifice of spiritual vision.

Jesus, the World Teacher, was speaking of this "eye" when he said, "The light of the body is the eye. If therefore thine eye be single, thy whole body shall be full of light." (Matt. 6:22)

Located at the center of the brow, it is emerald green when purified and has ninety-six petals (sometimes represented as two, as in the winged caduceus). Ideally, through the third eye, we should be able to anchor the vision of God, the vision of perfection.

Today, we live in a world of relativity and do not see or outpicture the absolute perfection of the God Self. When man was first created, before the descent of the soul into the planes of illusion (the Fall), he had the single-eyed vision of his original perfection in the third eye.

At the time of the Fall, when he partook of the fruit of the tree of the knowledge of relative good and evil, he fell into a state of duality. This is the propensity to see good and evil as relative qualities.

At the lowest point of the planetary evolution, some had lost the divine spark and walked the earth as animals. (It seems that Darwin was really a latecomer!) In actuality, mankind did not start as cavemen but descended into that state through neglect of devotion to the sacred fire of the heart and the misuse of the throat chakra and the third eye.

Since then, man has not been able to regain the fullness of his former faculties, although he may make great strides through the *exercise* of the heart chakra in devotion and meditation, the *exercise* of the throat chakra in the scientific use of the mantra or the dynamic decree of the Word, and the *exercise* of his spiritual vision by seeing the good in friend and foe alike.

The very fact that America has enjoyed such prosperity over the last two centuries has to do with the fact that its people have had the third-eye vision of a higher standard of excellence to make things happen.

Not only have we built a mighty nation of our own, but we have exported money and technology to almost every other nation on earth.

"Yes," you say, "but what about our economy? What about all of the unemployment?" Well, some of the nation's poor are those who have misused their chakras in the past, causing great harm to others, and are now experiencing the effects of causes they set in motion. But even this can be undone by the violet flame.

Karma, after all, is the iron law of cause and effect, more binding and all-encompassing than any earthly statute. This is not to disallow the negative and even diabolical influence that our past and present leaders have had on the economy and employment picture.

They have interfered with the free market by monopoly capitalism and federal regulation that has hurt a lot of good people who are the backbone of America. However, there is no injustice in the universe. Everyone must face the reaper in the form of his own personal karma. Everyone must ultimately pay the price for the misuse of the light of God—the oppressors as well as the oppressed. There are no exceptions.

The clearing of the third eye can be accomplished through meditation on perfect geometric forms, as well as through the raising of the energies of the lower chakras to the level of the third eye.

To begin, visualize a disc of light superimposed over your forehead, like a miner's light, only brighter. See it spinning and filling your vision center with light, flushing out the misqualified substance of the ages from your chakra, cleansing it until it is a brilliant emerald green.

As you are holding this picture in your mind's eye, give the following mantra of the science of the Word:

> O disc of light from heaven's height,
> Descend with all your perfection!
> Make our auras bright with freedom's light
> And the Master's love and protection!

Then call to your Christ Self and affirm:

> I AM, I AM beholding all,
> Mine eye is single as I call;
> Raise me now and set me free,
> Thy Holy Image now to be.

Clearing the third eye is a very important step in soul evolution, as it is directly correlated to the soul chakra. Whatever is seen through the third eye is also mirrored in the soul.

As a practical measure, third-eye vision can be improved through the cleansing of the colon and the physical body in general. Toxins accumulated in the blood and fatty tissue as well as in the colon are a direct hindrance to that vision. A balanced program of fasting on fresh vegetable or fruit juices, as well as distilled water and herb teas, is a good place to start.

14

THE SEAT-OF-THE-SOUL CHAKRA

The Chakra of Freedom

All the images seen with the third eye are reflected in the soul. The soul is anchored to the physical body through the seat-of-the-soul chakra, halfway between the navel and the base of the spine. This chakra governs the genetic code, heredity, and the manufacture of the seed and the egg. The seat of the soul has six petals and is violet in color.

Because of the very close relation between the soul and the third eye, the soul is easily damaged by impure and imperfect thoughtforms and images. This is especially true with some of today's art.

Color is especially important. Pastel light-emitting hues are better than loud or muddier shades, which are detrimental—as are amorphous shapes.

The pattern of Christ in the individual contains the geometry of the cosmos. Any dissonant or jagged art form is destructive to this geometry.

Long ago, advanced civilizations on the continent of Africa were brought down by perverted art and music, which eventually led to all forms of black magic and witchcraft being practiced there.

This has continued up to the present with voodoo, ritual murder, and sacrifice. These are extreme examples of the destruction of the soul chakra. Misuse of this and other chakras has caused vast devastation and, more than once, brought down a civilization or a continent.

The seat of the soul is the chakra of freedom. The movement toward "artistic freedom" in many cases actually accomplished the reverse. Because some modern art forms pervert the soul chakra, they take away from the freedom of the soul.

Parents with young children should be especially careful of what they allow their children to look upon and listen to. Some children today have never seen thoughtforms of perfection nor heard a chord of classical music.

It is vital that children have established within them certain archetypes, such as the Madonna and Child, the father figure in saints and heroes, flowers, and harmonious objects taken from nature in her unpolluted state. This instills in them the aspiration toward a path of self-discipline that can be won by striving for excellence in all of the four lower bodies.

Man is not unique in the possession of chakras. States and nations also have spiritual centers—highly concentrated energy focuses that govern the interaction of their people, their destiny and their vibrations, personal characteristics, language, accents, customs, and mannerisms.

People who have a certain karma to work out in a certain chakra will gravitate toward the corresponding city or state within their nation.

Los Angeles, the soul chakra of California as well as America, is the place of the greatest perversion of the freedom flame through the entertainment industry. (Does anyone really consider the *Texas Chainsaw Massacre* to be worthwhile art?) This perversion causes a distortion of the soul chakra of all the youth who view this and similar motion pictures.

Since the soul chakra is the creative center, whatever is created by those affected is then also distorted. As these youth grow up to be tomorrow's parents, educators, civic leaders, and film producers, it becomes a self-fulfilling prophecy. They look upon a distorted creation and then create more distortion in every field (even in the fertile field of consciousness of their own children). This, in turn, is looked upon by others and distorted further.

Indeed, you can see how each year the movies are more violent, delve deeper into the collective unconscious, and portray more hopelessness to an ever younger age group.

The only cure for this is for people who really care to begin purifying their soul chakras through meditation on images of beauty, symmetry, and higher consciousness. This is the first step.

Next, we must hold the visualization of the whirling disc, as with all of the other chakras, to flush out the substance that has built up with years of misuse of this vital center.

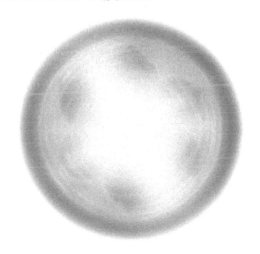

Use of the violet flame is essential, especially in this mechanistic society that is in large measure devoid of the pure thoughtforms and images necessary to maintain soul consciousness.

The mantra for use with this chakra is very short, but when repeated—and accompanied by visualization and the violet flame—it will have an extremely beneficial effect. Remember, "I AM" means "God in me is."

> Light expand, Light expand,
> Light expand, expand, expand!
> Light I AM, Light I AM,
> Light I AM, I AM, I AM!

15

THE CROWN CHAKRA

The Thousand-Petaled Lotus

The crown chakra is the chakra of illumination that regulates the mental faculties and memory. It is located at the top of the head and has 972 petals, a trait that has gained it the name of the "thousand-petaled lotus."

Yellow in color, the crown is the center through which we must attain God consciousness (the awareness of yourself as a part of God). A clogged crown chakra can ruin your memory just as surely as drug abuse. In fact, the taking of drugs is one of the primary factors that leads to the polluting of this chakra.

Mental density, the lack of a "clear head" when you need it most, "spacing out"—these are the effects of misqualified energy in the crown chakra.

On the opposite end of the scale are those who pervert the crown chakra by overuse of their mental faculties. There is nothing wrong, and in fact everything right, with having brain power. What we are concerned with here are the "eggheads"—people who believe that the only pursuits that matter are intellectual ones and who believe that those who are ignorant of the "higher" knowledge that they possess are naive and should have no say in the affairs of the world.

There are many in our government and political arena today, as well as in top positions in major corporations, who fit into this category. It is they who feel that we need to be controlled for our own good—that the little people of this world lack the ability to govern themselves. It is they who try to calm us with facts and figures, while what is left of our country either slowly slips away through economic decay or is "nuked" into oblivion.

These individuals, the mentalists, instead of developing an attunement with the higher mind through the crown chakra, are constantly releasing the poison of their lies and half-truths that stem from a corresponding relative perspective of good and evil in the misused third eye.

This comes out in the form of a violent orange/black/silver discharge that is wont to intimidate anyone of lesser sophistication. It seems that they are able, through the sheer force of their highly developed and highly manipulative mental bodies, to dupe the vast majority of the public.

If you are like most people in America, you have the earnest desire to see this country make it out of its current divisiveness—to regain its lost glory and fervor of patriotism that has carried it through revolution, civil war, and global conflict. Most of us

sincerely want to improve ourselves as well as our
surroundings. In this case, a little violet flame cou-
pled with the following mantra will go a long way.

> O Flame of Light bright and gold,
> O Flame most wondrous to behold,
> I AM in every brain cell shining,
> I AM Light's wisdom all divining.
> Ceaseless, flowing fount
> Of Illumination's flaming,
> I AM, I AM, I AM Illumination.

16

THE BASE-OF-THE-SPINE CHAKRA

The Mother Chakra

The final chakra we are concerned with is the Mother chakra. This is the base-of-the-spine chakra, referred to simply as the "base chakra." It derives its name from its location at the base of the spine. But it is also the base of our physical (and spiritual) temple. The God-quality of this chakra is purity. Its color is white and it has four petals, forming the foundation of the pyramid of being.

The life force of the base chakra is intended to be raised to the crown and the third eye by meditation on the I AM Presence. This will magnetize the energy upward.

As the life force, or Kundalini as it is called in the East, passes up through the channel connecting the chakras, it nourishes each one with the purity of the Mother light.

When the life force is perverted or abused, it contaminates all other chakras. Or, if it is spent entirely, there is nothing left to rise to activate the polarity of light in the other chakras. Disease, disintegration, decay, old age, and death are the price mankind pay for the misuse of the base-of-the-spine chakra.

Those who conserve the Mother light are the best performers and the most creative individuals in every field.

In our society, this is the chakra that has been most flagrantly abused through impurity in all forms. The mantra that will help rid your four lower bodies of impurity is called "I AM Pure":

By God's desire from on high,
Accepted now as I draw nigh,
Like falling snow with star-fire glow,
Thy blessed purity does bestow
Its gift of love to me.

I AM pure, pure, pure
By God's own word.
I AM pure, pure, pure,
O fiery sword.
I AM pure, pure, pure,
Truth is adored.

Descend and make me whole,
Blessed Eucharist, fill my soul.
I AM thy law, I AM thy light,
O mold me in thy form so bright!

Beloved I AM, beloved I AM, beloved I AM.

Now that you have cleared all of your chakras, go out and run! Go out and work that body until it won't work any more! You will feel an exhilaration you have never felt before, because now you have a complete program. Many professional athletes have discovered that they cannot survive in their training without the benefit of spiritual assistance.

Take, for example, the case of Toshihiko Seko, the winner of the Fukoka Marathon for three consecutive years. His entire life consists of training, both physically and spiritually. He is a devotee of Zen, and thanks to his trainer Kiyoshi Nakamura, he developed "Zensoho"—running with Zen.

According to Nakamura, "The idea is to clear your mind of everything and to let your body function naturally, undisturbed by thoughts." Nakamura has studied all of the world's religions for over forty years. "You can learn from them all, just like everything in life," he explains.

"We must study the Bible, scriptures, and all famous works. We must study nature—mountains, rivers, the stars, the sun and moon. All of them are our teachers."

Nakamura also subscribes to the belief that "physical training is only ten percent of the total preparation, the other ninety percent is mental."

In conclusion, many have come up with philosophies of training two or more of the four lower bodies while incorporating spiritual teachings from the world's religions. Seko is obviously utilizing a brand of this philosophy, with great results.

Why not take it a step further, then, and train all four of your bodies? Integrate them, clear out your chakras, breathe the prana of life, and gain maximum mastery over your total being.

I only hope that all who are aware of this teaching use it to its fullest. It is only through dedicated application of the Law that change can be effected. Just as the weekend or occasional runner will never make it to the marathon, so the dabbler in this science of the chakras will never make it to the spiritual olympics.

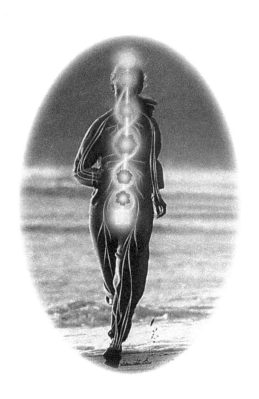

17

PRANA:
THE BREATH OF LIFE

Why is running a natural high? Why do you feel so invigorated after a brisk walk or a good hard workout? What is it that makes you think more clearly and feel like you're really alive?

Prana. The life energy that vitalizes all living things and controls all activities in the body—physical and spiritual, mental and sensory. Without it, blood won't circulate, organs won't function, and the brain won't do its job.

The concept of a universal energy force has been taught for many centuries and in many cultures. The Sanskrit term prana (meaning "breath" or "breath of life") has been compared to the *mana* of the Polynesians, to the Chinese ch'i, energy that circulates through the meridians detailed in the ancient science of acupuncture, to the Hebrew *ruach* ("spirit of life"), and to what scientists have in recent times called "bioplasma."

Prana is most easily absorbed into the body through the air, where it is found in its freest state. As you exercise—especially in fresh air and sunshine—you are inhaling, with each breath, air charged with this dynamic force. Like an electric current, it courses through an intricate system of nerve passages in the etheric body and is carried to every organ and part of the system, giving renewed strength and vigor.

Prana has its greatest concentration in the seven chakras, which serve as generating centers and focal points for this energy. The chakras regulate specific bodily functions, and at each of these energy centers the prana is collected and distributed to its destination.

Every activity—from muscle movement, to digestion, to thought itself—utilizes prana, and the supply needs to be constantly replenished to sustain good health. Unless enough fresh air reaches the lungs, for example, the venous blood (which accumulates waste from all parts of the body) cannot be purified or renewed with life. This poisonous waste matter, instead of being expelled, is then circulated through the body and poor health or disease ensues.

In fact, it is said that disease is due to an imbalance of prana. And some proponents of yoga believe that all sickness can be controlled when the proper flow of prana is restored. Along the same lines, in the West jogging has been used successfully as preventive medicine and even as therapeutic treatment for patients with heart problems.

Because all of the four lower bodies are interrelated, causes set into motion by prana are not limited to physical effects. A lack of prana can influence the mind and the emotions as well. Clinical tests have shown that there is a relationship between poor breathing and low IQ in children. And it's not hard to see how being confined to a stuffy room for too long can produce moodiness, depression, or apathy—instead of the buoyancy that an energy boost of fresh air and prana will provide.

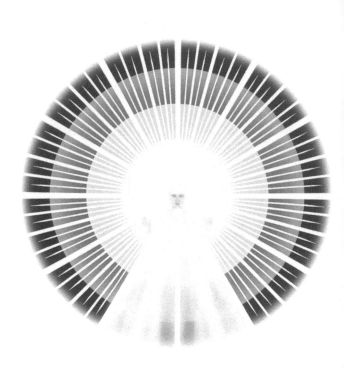

18

YOUR RELATIONSHIP TO GOD THROUGH CHRIST

Your Holy Christ Self is the still small voice of conscience that speaks to your soul with unerring direction, warns you of impending danger, and distinguishes between good and evil, right and wrong.

It is written that one day your soul will rise up and meet this Beloved One in the rapturous union that is the culmination of your life on earth. In this divine embrace you will recognize that there is no longer any need for separation from Christ—your Real Self. You need go out no more into outer darkness. You have found—you have become—your own Reality.

This union is known as the alchemical marriage. It is the mystical oneness with Christ experienced by the soul who has taken to heart Jesus' teaching: "Except ye eat the flesh of the Son of man, and drink his blood, ye have no life in you."

As you partake of the consciousness of your Christ Self day by day, you are entering into the communion of the "Son of man," whose Light is the true Light which lighteth every child of God.

For some, the saints and disciples of East and

West, the union with Christ has occurred before or during their final embodiment prior to the ascension. One with their Christ Self, they have accomplished on earth a great service to life by being lightbearers of the Word.

Jesus was the great exemplar of this union, for his oneness with Christ was so evident—the union of his humanity with his divinity so integral—that he walked the earth fully clothed upon with his Christ Self and fully the incarnation of the Word I AM THAT I AM—the mighty I AM Presence. He was the Three-in-One, the embodiment of the Trinity shown in the Chart of Your Divine Self. (See Fig. 2 on p. 29.)

The Chart shows that we are also destined to embody the fullness of the Godhead, as Paul so directed us when he said: "Let this mind be in you, which was also in Christ Jesus: who, being in the form of God, thought it not robbery to be equal with God."

Jesus' promise that the Father and the Son would take up their abode in those who love Christ and obey the Word opens the way to our discipleship under the same Law of the One whereby our Elder Brother attained his victory.

By this Christ in you and in me—the only hope of glory—we are made, as Paul says, "partakers of the inheritance of the saints in light."

Thus, the true inheritance of the children of God that they must now claim (for the false pastors have taken it from them) is the indwelling Son of God—the promised Lord Our Righteousness foretold by Jeremiah.

This beloved Christ Self known by Peter as "the hidden man of the heart" transforms our souls even as He exalts our highest hopes and loves, purifies the muddied stream of thought, forgives our tortuous feelings, transmutes our sins and sense of struggle, and is our strong advocate before the Father.

Becoming one with God through the Holy Christ Self is our reason for being on planet Earth. As Paul said—"Nevertheless I live; yet not I, but Christ liveth in me: and the life which I now live in the flesh I live by the faith of the Son of God. . . . "

The Chart of Your Divine Self illustrates what Jesus taught and the apostles knew: The son of man's unique relationship to God through Christ, the great mediator.

The Chart shows the relationship of the Person-hood of God the Father individualized in your mighty I AM Presence (the upper figure) and God the Son individualized in your Holy Christ Self (the middle figure) with your evolving soul conscious-ness—the son of man (the lower figure).[8]

This *son of manifestation* (the manifestation of God) is intended to be the temple of the Holy Spirit, as grace for grace the Paraclete is magnetized into your life by your heart's devotion to "your Lord and my Lord"—your Christ Self and my Christ Self. For we know and are convinced by the Law of the One that there is in Reality but one God, one LORD, and one Christ—albeit perceived individually and personally (as in the Chart) by each soul who has gone out from the Presence of God to serve the cause of Truth in the physical universe.

The Chart can be studied in the light of Jesus' own words:

"He that believeth on me, believeth not on me, but on him that sent me. And he that seeth me seeth him that sent me.

"I am come a light into the world, that whosoever believeth on me should not abide in darkness.

"And if any man hear my words, and believe not, I judge him not: for I came not to judge the world but to save the world. He that rejecteth me, and receiveth not my words, hath one that judgeth him: the Word that I have spoken, the same shall judge him in the last day.

"I have not spoken of myself; but the Father which sent me, he gave me a commandment, what

I should say, and what I should speak. And I know that his commandment is life everlasting: whatsoever I speak therefore, even as the Father said unto me, so I speak."

Even as Jesus proclaimed himself to be the Son of man sent by the Father as His messenger to deliver the Word of Christ, so the Chart reveals the great Truth that your mighty I AM Presence is the Father who sent you into the world to bear the Light of the Son, your own Christ Self, and to accomplish his Word and Work that through him you, the son of man, might have everlasting life.

As you descended from the Father and the Son, so one day you will ascend as Jesus did to the heart of the I AM Presence, one with your Christ Self. Jesus was teaching this principle to Nicodemus when he told him, "No man hath ascended up to heaven, but he that came down from heaven, even the Son of man [Soul of man] which is in heaven."[9]

We present these teachings with the prayer that through them you will come to know more of yourself in relationship to your Divine Reality shining just above you as the Glory of the Endless Day.

NOTES

1. Irving Oyle, *The Healing Mind* (Millbrae, Calif.: Celestial Arts, 1975), p. 42.

2. W. Edward Mann, *Orgone, Reich, and Eros* (New York: Simon & Schuster, 1973), p. 143.

3. Brian Inglis, *A History of Medicine* (Cleveland: World Publishing Co., 1965).

4. Aubrey Westlake, "Further Wanderings in the Radi-esthetic Field," *Journal of the British Society of Dowsers*, December 1951.

5. Margaret Goldsmith, *Franz Anton Mesmer* (Garden City, N. Y.: Doubleday, 1934).

6. Mikol Davis and Earle Lane, *The Rainbows of Life* (New York: Harper & Row, 1978).

7. John Joseph O'Neill, *Prodigal Genius: The Life of Nikola Tesla* (New York: I. Washburn, 1944).

8. The term "Son of man" (with a capital *S*), which Jesus used in reference to his own mission, defines the soul who has descended from the I AM Presence as the Son of God. Integrated with the Christ Self, this soul is now archetypically the presence of the Universal Soul of humanity. As in the life of Jesus, the Christ (Light)

of the one becomes the Christ (Light) for all. And the Son of man is perpetually one with and representing the Holy Christ Self of all souls evolving on earth. The term "son of man" (with a lowercase *s*) is applied to all souls who embody with the mission of bearing the light, balancing their karma, fulfilling their divine plan, and returning to God in the ritual of the ascension. The term "son of man" indicates that the potential exists for Divine Sonship through the path of personal Christhood—putting on day by day the garment of one's Lord, "eating his flesh and drinking his blood."

9. Jesus was the "son of man," but everyone who retains the divine spark, the threefold flame, is also the "son of man." The opportunity for joint heirship with Christ exists only in those who descended from above —from the I AM Presence. Hence they are called the I AM Race. Jesus also spoke of those who are "from beneath," a "generation of vipers" not of the Father but of the "devil" and his fallen angels, who are neither called nor chosen, a "race" that did not descend from the I AM Presence and therefore cannot ascend. This is the distinction Jesus is making to Nicodemus. Unlike certain modern theologians, the Master was willing to confront Good and Evil, and the Real and the unreal among men.

ABOUT
THE SUMMIT LIGHTHOUSE

Are you interested in the exploration of Reality, pursuing individual self-mastery, and finding those points shared in common by the mystical paths of the world's religions? The Summit Lighthouse, an endeavor of the great brotherhood of light, is a community of spiritual students around the world who share your interest. In pursuing these areas, we study and publish teachings of the ascended masters and use them to accelerate our spiritual path.

What are these teachings? Over the last 150 years, the ascended masters have again brought to mankind's attention the spiritual concepts of the ascension, karma and reincarnation, how to balance one's karma with the violet flame, finding twin flames and soul mates to accelerate fulfilling divine plans, soul liberation through the power of the spoken Word, prayer and meditation, and founding your point of identity with the reality of your I AM Presence—the divine spark within. Plus information on the long-rumored brotherhood of light that appears in times of need to help mankind.

What is this brotherhood of light? The Great White Brotherhood is comprised of men and women who mastered the fire of the heart, balanced their karma and fulfilled their dharma, finally ascended into the light of the presence of God. They return to help souls like you and me, their friends in past lives, to move beyond what we are used to and into that which we really are.

The Summit Lighthouse has its international headquarters at the Royal Teton Ranch, a beautiful land in the Rockies just north of Yellowstone National Park. If you are in the area, we welcome you to drop by for a chat and enjoy our new Yellowstone Hot Springs! This beautiful mineral-rich hot spring is located by the picturesque banks of the Yellowstone River.

Explore the free online lessons on karma, chakras, and the archangels, read an astounding story of Sanat Kumara, the Ancient of Days, view our free book offer, or sign-up for our free series of 16 ePearls on *The Chela and the Path* at:

SummitLighthouse.org

While you're there, learn more about the teachings of the ascended masters, the monthly *Pearls of Wisdom* subscription, the spiritual community at the Royal Teton Ranch, weekend seminars, quarterly conferences, summer retreats, the Keepers of the Flame Fraternity, or the Ascended Master Library and the study center nearest you.

For a free catalog of books, CDs and DVDs published by Summit University Press, go to:

www.SummitUniversityPress.com

CHAKRA LESSONS
HOW TO VITALIZE YOUR SEVEN ENERGY CENTERS

ACCESS YOUR RESOURCES FOR WHOLENESS
Based on the Science of the Body's Subtle Energy System

Sign up for 10 Free Online Lessons to help you vitalize your seven chakras!

Drawing from the wisdom of the world's spiritual traditions, you can nurture your soul through seven stages of personal growth. With these ten lessons you learn how to activate, balance, cleanse and master the seven major chakras using simple and effective spiritual exercises, visualizations and mantras.

ACCESS YOUR FREE LESSONS NOW

SummitLighthouse.org/free-spiritual-lessons/chakra-lessons

ELIZABETH CLARE PROPHET is a world-renowned author, spiritual teacher, and pioneer in practical spirituality. Her groundbreaking books have been published in more than thirty languages and over three million copies have been sold worldwide.

Part of this book is a condensation of a lecture by Elizabeth Clare Prophet delivered at the Summit University seminar, "Love Is the Key to the Mystery of the Word Incarnate within You."

Among her best-selling titles are *The Human Aura; The Science of the Spoken Word; Your Seven Energy Centers; The Lost Years of Jesus; The Art of Practical Spirituality;* and her successful Pocket Guides to Practical Spirituality series.

The Summit Lighthouse®
63 Summit Way, Gardiner, Montana 59030 USA

Se habla español.

TSLinfo@TSL.org
SummitLighthouse.org
www.ElizabethClareProphet.com
1-800-245-5445 / 406-848-9500